PLANTS
Let's Investigate

by Ruth Owen and Victoria Dobney

Consultant:
Nicky Waller

Ruby Tuesday Books

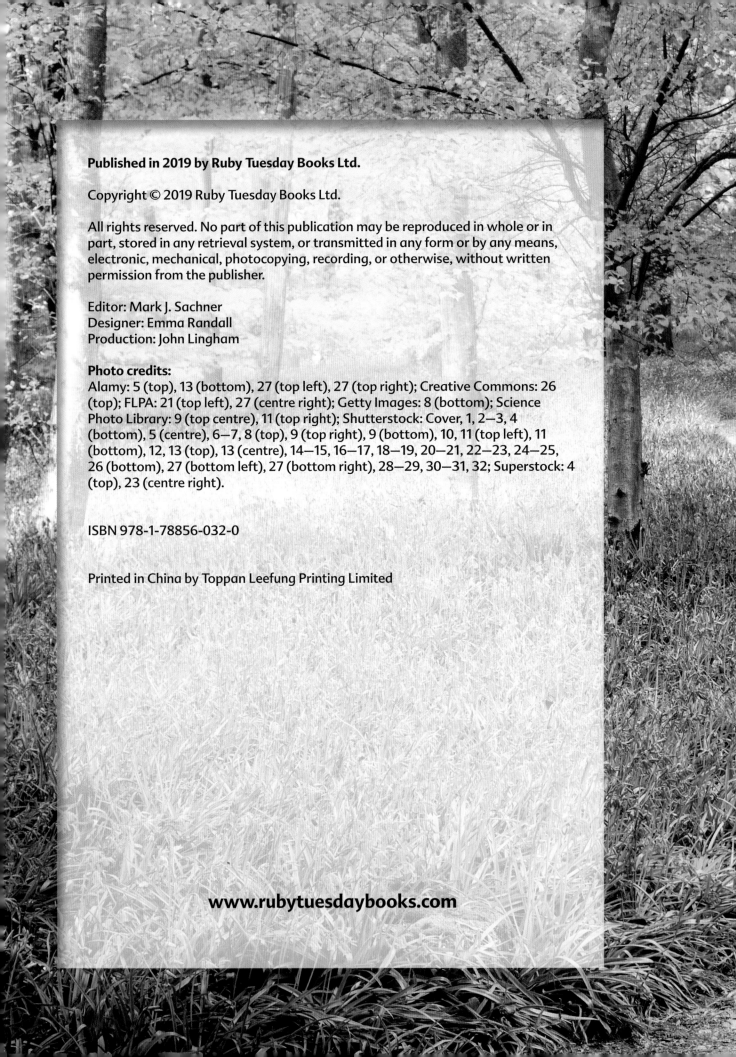

Published in 2019 by Ruby Tuesday Books Ltd.

Copyright © 2019 Ruby Tuesday Books Ltd.

Editor: Mark J. Sachner
Designer: Emma Randall
Production: John Lingham

Photo credits:
Alamy: 5 (top), 13 (bottom), 27 (top left), 27 (top right); Creative Commons: 26 (top); FLPA: 21 (top left), 27 (centre right); Getty Images: 8 (bottom); Science Photo Library: 9 (top centre), 11 (top right); Shutterstock: Cover, 1, 2—3, 4 (bottom), 5 (centre), 6—7, 8 (top), 9 (top right), 9 (bottom), 10, 11 (top left), 11 (bottom), 12, 13 (top), 13 (centre), 14—15, 16—17, 18—19, 20—21, 22—23, 24—25, 26 (bottom), 27 (bottom left), 27 (bottom right), 28—29, 30—31, 32; Superstock: 4 (top), 23 (centre right).

ISBN 978-1-78856-032-0

Printed in China by Toppan Leefung Printing Limited

www.rubytuesdaybooks.com

Contents

The download button shows there are free worksheets or other resources available. Go to:
www.rubytuesdaybooks.com/scienceKS2

Plants for the Future

On a Norwegian island in the Arctic Ocean, there is a high-security building deep inside an ice-covered mountain. To gain entry, people must pass through many locked doors. What is taking place here?

This is the Svalbard Global **Seed Vault**. And inside, scientists are saving seeds!

The Global Seed Vault stores seeds from around the world. In the future, **climate change**, plant diseases or the destruction of natural **habitats** could kill off some **species** of plants. If some of the seeds of those plants are protected, they can be taken from the vault and grown again.

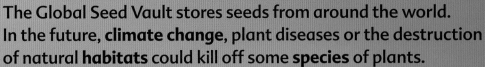

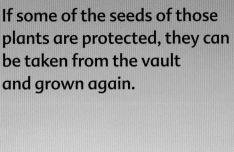

Polar Protection

The seed vault was built at Svalbard because this area has no earthquakes that could damage the collection. The seeds are kept in freezers, but being in a naturally icy place is also an added protection. Polar bears prowl the icy mountain and the scientists joke that they are the vault's security guards!

Scientists inside the seed vault

About 500 seeds from a plant species are wrapped in small foil packets. Then the seeds are sealed inside boxes and stored at a temperature of −18°C. Just like frozen food in your home freezer, the frozen seeds will stay fresh until they are defrosted.

Foil packet of seeds

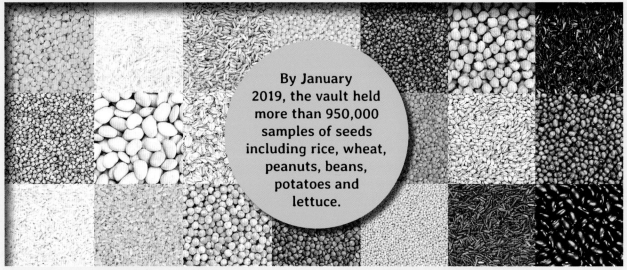

By January 2019, the vault held more than 950,000 samples of seeds including rice, wheat, peanuts, beans, potatoes and lettuce.

Use By Dates

Scientists think that some types of seeds will survive in the vault for thousands of years. Others will not last that long and will die. Before a batch of seeds gets too old, it will be taken from the vault and planted. Then fresh seeds will be gathered from the plants that have grown and put back into storage.

Let's Talk!

All plants are important, but which five plant seeds would you put into the vault? Why did you choose these species?

Protecting seeds and the wonderful plant life on Earth is very important work. People and animals need plants as food. Also, plants make the **oxygen** we need to breathe.

Plants are essential for life on Earth.

Roots

Every part of a plant has a special function (or job to do) to help the plant survive and reproduce.

Let's start at the bottom of the plant with **roots**.

The roots of most plants grow underground in soil. Thin, hairlike roots sprout from a plant's thicker, or main, roots.

The hairlike roots take in water from the soil. The water then travels through the thicker roots up into the plant's stem.

Some plants have lots of roots that spread out in all directions under the soil.

A tree's stem is called a trunk.

Roots

Some plants have one thick main root, called a taproot, that grows straight down into the soil.

Carrot plant

Taproot

Hairlike roots

The orange bit we eat is a carrot plant's taproot.

To be healthy, plants need **nutrients**. For example, nitrogen is a nutrient that helps plants grow lots of leaves. Nutrients are found in soil **dissolved** in water. Most plants take in nutrients when they take in water. The nutrients help a plant produce leaves, flowers, **fruits** and seeds.

Kapok tree

Another function of a plant's roots is to hold it in the soil and keep it upright. Without roots a plant could be blown over when it's windy. As its branches, leaves, flowers or fruits grow and get heavy, a plant might topple over if it didn't have roots.

Buttress Roots

Kapok trees grow in rainforests and can be taller than a 20-storey building. Sometimes rainforest soil is shallow, so a tree's roots can't grow down very deep. Kapok trees grow buttress roots above ground that spread out and stop the giant trees falling over.

Buttress roots

A kapok tree's buttress roots may grow for 30 metres over the ground.

Let's Investigate

Can roots find water?

Equipment:
- A plastic container that is about 10 cm deep and 15 cm long
- Potting soil
- 6 bean seeds
- A watering can
- A marker pen
- A notebook and pen

Method:

1 Fill the container with soil up to about 2 cm below the rim.

2 Place three seeds on the soil at opposite ends of the container. Cover the seeds with a thin layer of soil.

3 Place on a sunny windowsill. Water regularly to keep the soil moist.

4 Once the seedlings are about 3 cm high, choose the strongest seedling from each row and carefully pull out the others. Label the plants A and B.

5 Every other day, water the soil in seedling A's half of the container, leaving plant B's dry.

What do you think will happen to seedling B's roots? Write down your predictions in your notebook.

6 After four weeks gently scoop the soil away from the plants so you can see their roots.

What do you observe about the roots of the two seedlings? What do you think has happened and why? Did your predictions match what happened?

Stems

A plant's stems are like its framework or skeleton.

Most plants have a main stem that grows out of the ground. Thinner stems grow from the main stem. The function of a plant's stems is to transport water and nutrients from the roots to the leaves, flowers or fruits.

A tree's thin stems are called branches. They connect to even thinner stems called twigs, where the leaves grow.

A Record-Breaking Plant

A plant's main stem can be thin and just a centimetre tall, or massive like the trunk of a giant sequoia tree. The biggest tree in the world (by volume) is a giant sequoia named the General Sherman tree. The huge tree is about 2500 years old.

Scientists estimate General Sherman weighs about 1.2 million kilograms – the same as 350 elephants.

The tree's bark is up to 1 metre thick.

General Sherman is 84 metres tall.

GENERAL SHERMAN

A plant's stems contain tubes called **xylem** (*zye-lem*) and **phloem** (*flow-em*).

The xylem tubes carry water and nutrients from the roots through the plant's stems to its leaves.

Inside its leaves, a plant makes food for **energy** (see pages 10–11). The phloem tubes carry this food from the leaves to wherever it is needed inside the plant.

This image shows a slice from a nasturtium stem. It is about 100 times bigger than real life. The image was taken by a powerful scanning electron microscope.

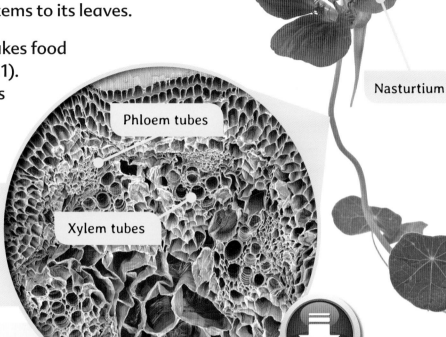

Phloem tubes

Xylem tubes

Nasturtium

Rainbow Stems

The bark on the trunk of a rainbow gum tree (or eucalyptus tree) peels off in patches. At first the fresh bark underneath is green. Then it changes to bright colours such as red, orange or purple.

Bark is a tough covering that grows on a tree's trunk and branches. Bark protects a tree from being harmed by rain, snow or hot sun, and from being eaten by animals.

Stems for Storage

Baobab (*bay-uh-bab*) trees grow in hot, dry deserts. When rain does fall, the tree takes in as much water as possible and stores it in its trunk. A large baobab tree can hold enough water to fill about 50 baths!

Baobab trees are also known as bottle trees.

Leaves

When a plant takes in nutrients, it's a little like you taking some vitamins. But you also need food to help you grow, have energy and be healthy. It's the same for plants. They need both nutrients and food.

Plants make their own sugary food called glucose. They do this inside their leaves using sunlight, water and a **gas** from the air called **carbon dioxide**. This process is called **photosynthesis**.

Photosynthesis takes place with the help of a green substance called **chlorophyll** that plants make in their leaves. It's chlorophyll that gives leaves their green colour.

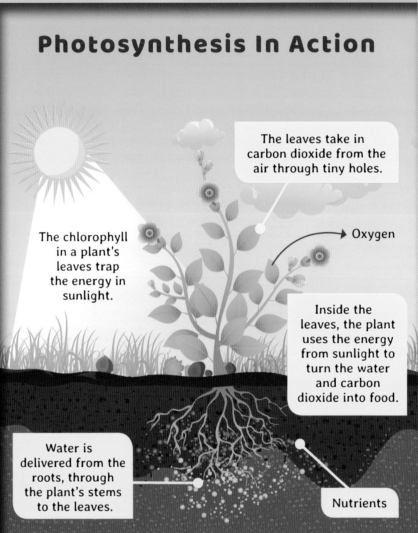

Photosynthesis In Action

The leaves take in carbon dioxide from the air through tiny holes.

The chlorophyll in a plant's leaves trap the energy in sunlight.

Oxygen

Inside the leaves, the plant uses the energy from sunlight to turn the water and carbon dioxide into food.

Water is delivered from the roots, through the plant's stems to the leaves.

Nutrients

Let's Talk!

Take a close-up look at a leaf and you'll see its veins. What is the function of the veins?
(The answer is at the bottom of the page.)

Veins

ANSWER: The veins are like tiny tubes that carry water from the stem into the leaf.

Breathe Deep, Thank a Plant!

During photosynthesis, plants make oxygen. They release this gas into the air through the tiny holes on their leaves. Without plants making the oxygen we need, people and animals would not be able to breathe.

A stoma on a rose leaf

The tiny, mouth-like holes on a leaf are called stomata. A single hole is a stoma. The stomata are usually on the underside of a leaf and can only be seen with a microscope.

Making Food, Helping the Planet

When vehicles burn petrol or diesel and power plants burn gas or coal to make electricity, carbon dioxide is released into the air. Too much carbon dioxide in the air is helping to trap the Sun's heat on Earth, causing the climate to warm up. During photosynthesis plants help the planet by removing harmful carbon dioxide from the air.

Let's Investigate

What happens if a plant doesn't get enough light?

We will work scientifically by using two identical plants and controlling how much light each one gets.

Equipment:
- Two identical potted plants
- Two saucers
- A small watering can

Method:

1 Stand each plant in a saucer. This will catch any excess water.

2 Put one plant inside a dark cupboard and the other on a sunny windowsill.

3 Water the plants regularly in equal amounts to keep the soil moist.

What do you think will happen to the plant in the cupboard? Write down your predictions.

4 Check on your plants every three to four days and record any changes you observe.

5 Continue for three weeks, noting changes to each plant.

Do the plants look different? In what ways? Did your results match your predictions?

Bug-Catching Bog Plants

Wetlands are habitats that are home to many different types of plants.

In a wetland there may be streams, rivers, ponds or lakes and the land is often underwater. Wetland plants grow in the water and on the wet, soggy land. One type of wetland is a peat bog.

A peat bog habitat

Peat soil

What Is a Peat Bog?

A peat bog gets its name from a special type of soil called peat. This type of soil forms when dead plants don't fully decay, or rot away. Instead, layers of partly rotted plant material build up over thousands of years to create a dark, stodgy soil.

The soil in a peat bog often contains very few nutrients for plants to take in with their roots. To survive, some bog plants have **adapted** to get nutrients in another way — by catching insects!

Sticky Sundews

A **carnivorous** sundew plant's leaves are covered with tiny stalks that produce a sticky glue. The plant's trick is that the glue smells like sweet **nectar**. When an insect smells the fake nectar, it zooms in for a meal and gets stuck!

Sundew plants

Leaf

Fly stuck in glue

It's too late for this fly! One leg gets stuck, then another. As the insect struggles to escape, the leaf curls around it. Then the leaf releases juices that dissolve the fly. As the insect dissolves, the leaf **absorbs** nutrients from its body.

Sundew plant leaf

Glue-covered stalks

Bugs and Sunlight

Carnivorous plants catch insects and other small animals to get nutrients. They also make sugary food in their leaves through photosynthesis.

The leaves are absorbing nutrients from the bodies of the tiny flies.

Deadly Sticky Butterworts

The leaves of a butterwort plant are covered with shiny drops of glue that look like water or nectar. When a hungry insect lands on a leaf, it gets trapped in the glue. Tiny hairs on the leaves produce the glue and other hairs release the juices that turn the insect into a soupy mush.

Flowers

Many types of plants, including trees, are flowering plants. The function of a plant's flowers is to produce seeds for **reproduction**.

A flower has male and female parts that each have a job to do.

A Lily flower

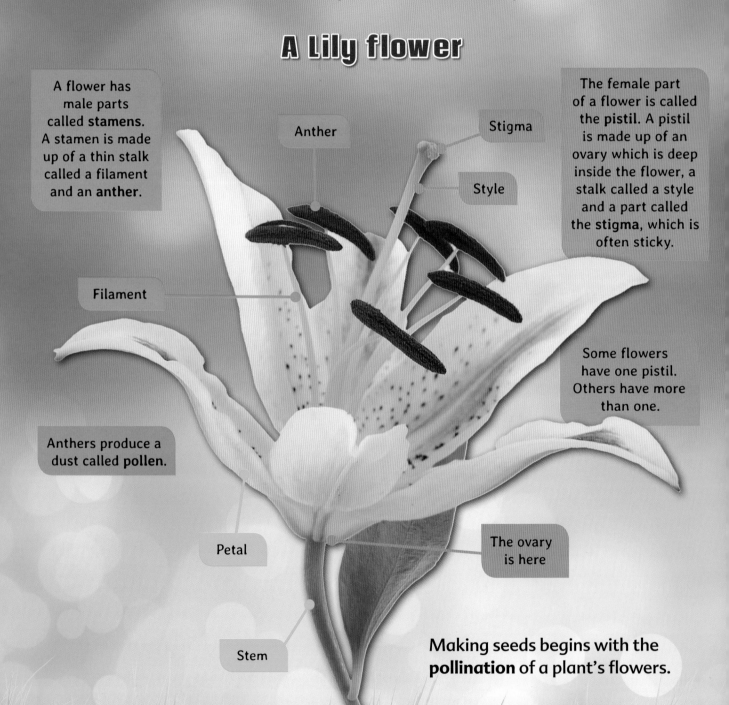

A flower has male parts called **stamens**. A stamen is made up of a thin stalk called a filament and an **anther**.

Anther

Stigma

Style

The female part of a flower is called the **pistil**. A pistil is made up of an ovary which is deep inside the flower, a stalk called a style and a part called the **stigma**, which is often sticky.

Filament

Anthers produce a dust called **pollen**.

Some flowers have one pistil. Others have more than one.

Petal

The ovary is here

Stem

Making seeds begins with the **pollination** of a plant's flowers.

Pollination in Action

The pollen made by the anthers of one flower must be carried to the stigma of another flower of the same species. How?

Pollen can be carried by the wind or on the body of a **pollinator** such as a bee, butterfly, moth, wasp, fly, bird or bat.

To attract pollinators, flowers produce nectar that the animals want to eat.

A honeybee lands on a flower and crawls around searching for nectar. Pollen from the flower's anthers sticks to its fuzzy body.

When it's finished feeding, the bee flies to a different flower. The pollen goes too.

As the bee searches for nectar, some pollen brushes off onto that flower's stigma.

A flower's petals are often colourful or scented to attract pollinators.

Pollen

If pollen from a poppy's anthers is carried to the stigma of a lily, the lily won't be able to use that pollen to make seeds. Flowers can only be pollinated by pollen from a plant of the same species.

Once pollen from one flower lands on the stigma of another, the flower is pollinated.

Seeds

Once a flower has been pollinated, the next stage in making seeds is fertilisation.

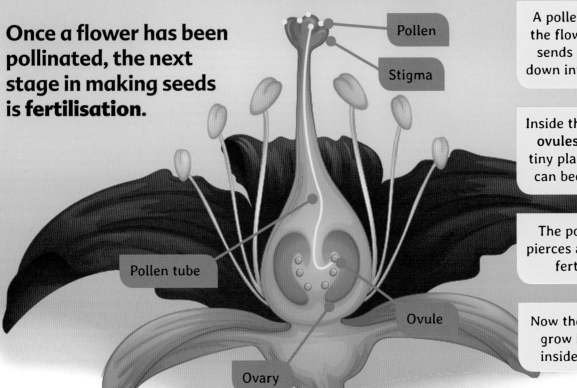

Pollen

Stigma

Pollen tube

Ovule

Ovary

A pollen grain on the flower's stigma sends a tiny tube down into the ovary.

Inside the ovary are **ovules**, which are tiny plant parts that can become seeds.

The pollen tube pierces an ovule and fertilises it.

Now the ovule can grow into a seed inside the ovary.

What Are Fruits?

As the seeds grow, the flower's ovary swells up and becomes a protective covering called a fruit. When we say "fruit" we think of something like an apple or a peach. But a fruit is actually any kind of outer layer that protects seeds as they grow.

As the fruit forms, the flower dies.

Poppy seeds are growing inside this seedpod, or fruit.

This is a lily fruit. It is also called a seedpod.

Tomato seeds inside a soft, protective fruit.

The heads of some flowers are not just one single flower. They are formed from hundreds of tiny flowers all growing together. Sunflower heads grow in this way.

The sunflower's centre is made up of hundreds of individual tiny flowers.

Each tiny flower has male and female parts.

Stigma

Anther

Ovary

The outer yellow petals attract pollinators.

Seeds forming

Once each flower is pollinated, it grows into a seed.

Let's Investigate

Seeds need water, nutrients, air, sunlight and room to grow. Most seeds also need soil. But what happens if too many seedlings try to grow in the same spot?

What happens if seedlings have too much competition?

Equipment:
- 2 small, empty, clean yogurt pots
- A marker pen
- Potting compost
- Bean seeds
- 2 saucers
- A tablespoon

Method:

1. Ask an adult to pierce three holes in the bottom of each yogurt pot for drainage. Label the pots A and B.

2. Fill each pot three-quarters full with potting compost.

3. Place 5 bean seeds on top of the soil in pot A and 2 seeds in pot B.

4. Cover the seeds with more soil. Stand each pot on a saucer and place in a sunny spot.

5. Give each pot a tablespoon of water every day. When the seedlings emerge, remove the weakest seedling from pot B, leaving just one plant.

How will the seedling in pot B be different to the seedlings in pot A as it grows? Write down your predictions.

6. Keep watering the seedlings each day. Observe them for one month.

Record your results. Did they match your predictions?

Seeds on the Move

To avoid competition, many seeds move to a new growing place away from their parent plant. How do they do this?

On the Move in Poo

The fruits around seeds become food for animals. An animal's body digests the soft fruit but the hard seeds pass through. The seeds then leave the animal's body in its poo, often far from the parent plant.

A blackbird eating berries.
A berry is a fruit with a seed inside.

Animal Gardeners

Squirrels eat acorns, which are oak tree seeds. In autumn, squirrels collect acorns and bury them in soil. When there's not much food around in winter, they dig up their stored seeds. Squirrels don't find all the buried acorns, however, and some grow into oak trees.

Hooked on You

Burdock plants produce balls of seeds called burrs. Each seed in a burr has a tiny hook. When an animal brushes past the burr, the seeds hook into its fur or feathers and hitch a ride away from their parent plant.

A New Plant

Once a seed settles in some soil it may wait until spring to start growing.

Tiny leaves sprout and begin making food with water, carbon dioxide and sunlight.

A seedling or shoot grows and pushes up above ground.

Seed

The roots deliver water and nutrients to the seedling.

If seedlings try to grow too close to each other or their parent plant, there may not be enough water and nutrients to go around. The bigger parent plant may also block out sunlight.

Floating Away

Lotus flowers grow in ponds and lakes. Each flower grows its seeds in a hard fruit called a pod. When the seeds are ready, the pod's stem bends down and the seeds fall from the pod into the water. Then the seeds float to a new growing place.

A lotus flower seedpod forming

Seeds inside a pod

Up, Up and Away

A dandelion flower produces up to 400 seeds. Each seed has a fluffy parachute to catch the wind and help the tiny seed float to a new home.

Comparing Life Cycles

A tomato plant and a saguaro cactus are both flowering plants. Their life cycles are very different, though.

The seeds inside the tomatoes get eaten or they are collected and planted to make new plants.

A gardener or farmer plants tomato seeds in soil.

After two weeks, a seedling appears. One month later and the young plant is 25 cm tall.

A Tomato Plant's Life Cycle

A tomato plant lives for about six to eight months. People all over the world grow tomato plants and eat their fruits.

At three months old, the plant is 1 metre tall. It grows yellow flowers.

Bees and other insects visit the plant to drink nectar.

When autumn comes, the final fruits are picked. The plant shrivels and dies.

As the fruits swell and become ripe, they change colour from green to yellow to red.

Once the flowers are pollinated, seeds start to grow inside green fruits.

A Saguaro Cactus's Life Cycle

Saguaro cactuses grow in the Sonoran Desert in Arizona, USA. They can grow to be 18 metres tall and live for up to 200 years.

A tiny black saguaro cactus seed falls onto the sandy desert soil inside a bird poo. A seedling starts to grow. After 10 years, the little plant is just 3 cm tall.

Saguaro cactus seedling

After 70 years, the cactus is 2 metres tall.

At 70 to 100 years old, the cactus starts to grow arms, or branches. It also starts to grow flowers in the spring.

Gila woodpecker

Each flower blooms for just 24 hours. Pollinators, such as bats, birds and bees, visit the flowers to feed on nectar.

Curved-billed thrasher bird

Juicy red fruits grow from the flowers. Each fruit contains about 2000 seeds. Animals feed on the fruits and seeds.

21

Cones and Spores

Some plants do not grow flowers. They have other ways of reproducing.

A group of plants called conifers produce their seeds inside **cones**. A conifer, such as a pine tree or giant sequoia tree, grows male and female cones.

The male cones produce pollen, which they release into the air.

Pollen

Male pine cone

Female pine cone

Scales

The female cones produce ovules between their woody scales. The pollen lands on the ovules and fertilises them. Then the ovules grow into seeds.

Pine tree seeds

When the seeds are grown, the female cone's scales open out fully and the seeds fall to the ground.

Fern Reproduction

Ferns do not grow flowers or produce seeds. They reproduce by releasing tiny, dust-like **spores** that fall to the ground. A spore becomes a heart-shaped growth called a prothallus that grows in the soil. The prothallus has sperm and an egg. The sperm fertilises the egg and then the tiny prothallus starts to grow into a new fern plant.

Fern spores form in a case called a sorus on the underside of a fern's fronds, or leaves.

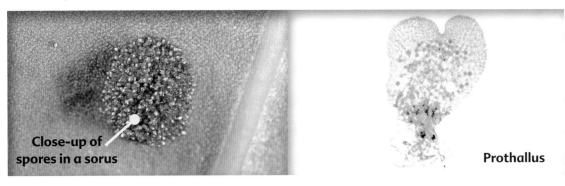

Close-up of spores in a sorus

Prothallus

A carpet-like covering of moss on a log or rock is made up of thousands of plants growing close together.

Capsules of spores

Each individual moss plant has a single stem and tiny leaves.

Moss Reproduction

Some moss plants are males that have sperm and some are females that have eggs. A male plant releases sperm into some water, such as a raindrop. The sperm swim to female plants and fertilise their eggs. After fertilisation, a female moss grows a capsule filled with spores that are released into the air. Each microscopic spore can become a new moss plant.

Asexual Reproduction

In the world of plants there are two types of reproduction — sexual reproduction and asexual reproduction. Let's investigate!

For sexual reproduction to take place, two parents are needed. For example:

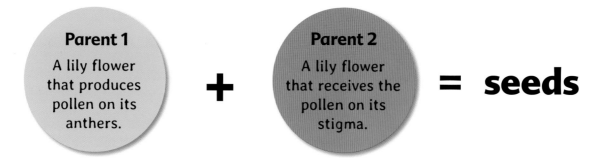

Parent 1
A lily flower that produces pollen on its anthers.

+

Parent 2
A lily flower that receives the pollen on its stigma.

= seeds

Some plants, however, are able to reproduce asexually. This means they can produce new plants all on their own. How?

Roots grow down into the ground from the bulb.

New Plants from Bulbs: Daffodils

Like other flowering plants, daffodils can reproduce sexually by producing seeds. But they can also reproduce asexually from their bulbs. The bulb is an underground store of water and food that the plant uses as it grows. Under the ground the bulb splits, forming small bulbs called bulblets. Each bulblet will become a new plant.

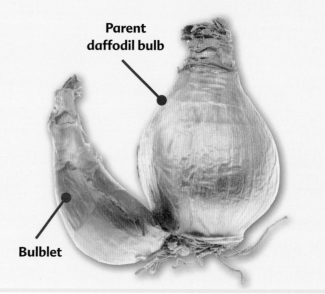

Parent daffodil bulb

Bulblet

New Plants from Tubers: Potato Plants

A potato plant grows leaves and flowers. It makes lots of food with its leaves. It makes so much food that under the ground it forms fat tubers for storing the spare food. We call the tubers potatoes.

Potato plant

Tubers (or potatoes)

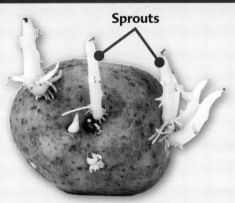

Sprouts

A potato plant can produce seeds, but it can also reproduce asexually from its tubers. Have you ever noticed an old potato growing little sprouts? If that potato is planted in soil, the sprouts will become new potato plants.

New Plants from Runners: Strawberry Plants

Strawberry plants grow flowers, fruits and seeds. But they also make new plants asexually by sending out shoots called runners. At the end of each runner are roots and small leaves.

The roots grow down into the soil and the runner becomes a whole new plant.

Parent strawberry plant

New plant

Runner

Strawberry seeds grow on the outside of the fruit.

Strawberry flower

Crucial Conservation

You may recognise Chris Packham (CBE) from the television, or even know of his work as a **conservationist** and **campaigner**.

In 2018, Chris led the UK Bioblitz campaign. Volunteers recorded the state of 50 wildlife sites across the UK. They did this by counting and recording the different species of mammals, birds, insects, fungi and plants they saw at each site.

The Bioblitz data will be used as a benchmark to compare how things might change in the future.

Conservation:
the protection of plants, animals and natural habitats.

The **Bioblitz** **campaign** recorded information on **4828** different species.

Wood anemones are one of the plants counted during the Bioblitz.

People's Manifesto For Wildlife

Chris Packham has also launched *A People's Manifesto For Wildlife*. This is a report in which Chris highlights concerns about the UK's landscape and wildlife. The manifesto includes suggestions for many changes. These include replanting hedgerows and taking better care of them, creating an Environment Act similar to the Human Rights Act and reintroducing wild animals to habitats where they once lived.

Endangered Plants

We think of endangered species as always being animals. But many plants are in danger, too, and face extinction.

Ley's Whitebeam
(Sorbus leyana)

Type of plant: Tree

Habitat: On steep limestone cliff sides in the Brecon Beacons, Wales.

Status: Critically endangered in the UK. There are only 17 trees left in the wild (Summer 2019).

- In the past, quarrying (cutting rock) in the trees' habitat destroyed many trees.
- Animals graze on the trees.

Spreading Bellflower
(Campanula patula)

Type of plant: Flowering plant

Habitat: Meadows and open woodlands in Europe

Status: Critically endangered in the UK.

- Weedkillers used on roadsides and railway verges kill this plant.
- The reduction of coppicing (cutting trees back to a stump to encourage new shoots to grow) means that many woodlands are now overcrowded and too dark for this plant to grow.

Saving Hedgerows

Hedgerows are vital habitats for plants and they give animals homes, hiding places and food. In the UK, about 300,000 kilometres of hedgerows have been destroyed in the last 60 years.

A farmer cutting hedgerows

The Problems:

- Modern farming has led to the destruction of some hedgerows to create big fields that are easier to plant and harvest with large machines.
- Hedgerows are destroyed when new roads are built.
- Hedgerows are often cut back too much by machines just to make them look tidy. This can kill nesting birds and other wildlife.

A dunnock nest in a hedgerow

- Plants that grow berries and nuts (such as blackberries and hazelnuts) are cut down before they are fully grown and can be eaten by wildlife.

A hazel dormouse eating blackberries

What Can Be Done?

- Replant new hedgerows in places where they have been removed.
- Replant and replace old hedgerows as they die out.
- Put in place rules to stop hedgerow cutting during nesting times, and at times when plants are producing flowers or fruits.

Classifying Plants

Scientists have discovered and named almost 400,000 different species of plants. They keep track of them all using a system called classification.

Classification means to sort different species of living things into groups according to their similarities and differences. One way plants can be grouped is as flowering plants or non-flowering plants.

**Dandelion
(flowering plant)**

**Hart's tongue fern
(non-flowering plant)**

When a new plant is discovered, scientists can compare different features of the plant to the plants in different classification groups. This helps them learn what type of plant it is.

Carl Linnaeus

Carl Linnaeus was a Swedish botanist (plant scientist) and zoologist (animal scientist) who lived in the 1700s. He created a systematic way to classify living things. He also invented a way to name them called the binomial naming system.

Under this system, every living thing is given a two-word Latin name. The first part is the genus (or group) name. The second word is the species name. For example:

Quercus robur = English oak
Quercus kelloggii = California black oak

There are about 600 different species of oak tree and each species has its own binomial name. Naming plants in this way makes it easier for scientists to communicate even if they all speak different languages and have different words for oak tree.

Classification Key

Classification keys are used to sort living things according to their characteristics. They are made up of questions with a "yes" or "no" answer. Have a go at sorting these leaves using the classification key below to discover what tree they come from.

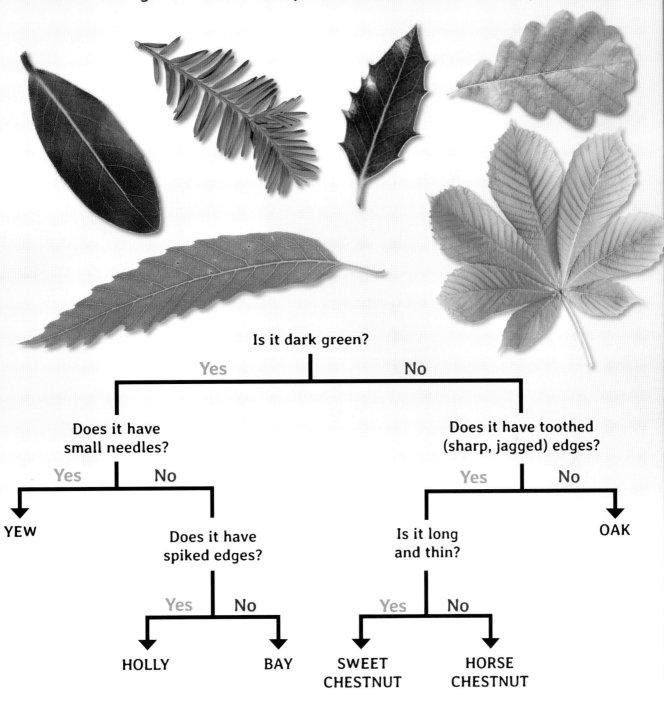

Is it dark green?

Yes | No

Does it have small needles?

Yes → **YEW**

No → **Does it have spiked edges?**

Yes → **HOLLY**

No → **BAY**

Does it have toothed (sharp, jagged) edges?

Yes → **Is it long and thin?**

No → **OAK**

Yes → **SWEET CHESTNUT**

No → **HORSE CHESTNUT**

Method:

1. Choose a leaf to classify and start with the first question at the top of the classification key.

2. Follow the branches for either "yes" or "no" and then ask yourself the next question.

3. When you have reached the last question, you will know what tree the leaf came from.

Glossary

absorb
To soak up or take in.

adapt
To change in order to be successful in a particular habitat or to be suitable for a particular way of life. For example, a baobab tree has adapted to desert life by storing water in its trunk.

anther
A male part of a flower that makes pollen.

carbon dioxide
A colourless gas in the air that plants use to make food. When humans and animals breathe out, they release carbon dioxide into the air.

carnivorous
Meat-eating.

chlorophyll
The substance in leaves that traps sunlight and uses it to make a plant's food. Chlorophyll gives plants their green colour.

climate change
A gradual change in temperatures on Earth — for example, the current warming of temperatures caused by a build-up of greenhouse gases (such as carbon dioxide, methane and nitrous oxide) in the atmosphere.

cone
The fruit of a coniferous plant that produces either pollen or seeds.

conservationist
A person who does work to protect plants, animals and natural habitats.

dissolve
A process in which a solid mixes with a liquid and becomes part of it. For example, if you mix salt (a solid) with water (a liquid), the salt dissolves and you get salt water.

energy
The force that allows things to move and happen. Plants use energy from sunlight to make a sugary food. Plants also create energy for animals to use.

fertilisation
In plants, the process in which a pollen grain enters an ovule and makes it ready to grow into a seed. Or when a moss or fern plant's sperm fertilises an egg so that it is ready to grow into a new plant.

fruit
A protective case or covering in which seeds can grow.

function
The special purpose, or job, that something has. For example, the functions of plant roots are to take in water and nutrients and hold a plant upright in the soil.

gas
A substance that floats in air and is neither a liquid nor a solid. Most gases, such as carbon dioxide, are invisible.

habitat
The natural home of an animal or plant. A garden, woodland or desert are all examples of a habitat.

nectar
A sweet sugary liquid produced by plants to attract insects and other animals.

nutrients
Substances needed by a plant or animal to help it live and grow. For example, nitrogen is a nutrient that helps plants grow healthy leaves.

ovule
A tiny part of a plant that grows into a seed once it is fertilised by pollen.

oxygen
A gas in the air that has no colour and no smell. Oxygen is produced by plants. People and animals breathe oxygen.

phloem
Tubes inside a plant that carry food from the leaves through the stems to wherever it is needed inside the plant.

photosynthesis
The process by which plants make food. *Photosynthesis* comes from the words *photo,* which means "light", and *synthesis,* which means "putting together". Using light, plants put together water and carbon dioxide to make sugary glucose.

pistil
The female reproductive part of a flower that includes the ovary, style and stigma.

pollination
The movement of pollen from the anther of a flower to a stigma.

pollinator
An animal that carries pollen from one flower to another.

reproduction
Making more of something. For example, a sunflower reproduces by making seeds that will grow into more sunflowers.

roots
Parts of plants that are usually under the ground in soil and take in water and nutrients. Roots spread out in soil to hold a plant in place.

seed
A part of a plant that contains all the material needed to grow a new plant.

species
One type of living thing. The members of a species look alike and can reproduce together.

spore
A tiny dust-like part of a plant, such as a moss or fern, that can grow into a new plant.

stamen
The male reproductive part of a flower that includes the filament and anther.

stigma
A female part of a flower where pollen must land in order for pollination to happen.

vault
A large room or other space that's used for storage. A vault is usually underground.

xylem
Tubes inside a plant that carry water and nutrients from the roots through the stems and to the leaves, flowers and fruit.

Index